The Level System

A Natural Drum Technique Method for Developing Control of Accents and Dynamics

Jeffrey W. Johnson

Alfred Music Publishing Co., Inc.
16320 Roscoe Blvd., Suite 100
P.O. Box 10003
Van Nuys, CA 91410-0003

alfred.com

ISBN-10: 0-7390-8664-2
ISBN-13: 978-0-7390-8664-3

Table of Contents

Introduction

The purpose of this book is to introduce the reader to the level system, a method of performance that allows the drummer to transition instantly between accented and unaccented notes. The level system is unlike most other methods of drumming because the hands always prepare for the upcoming note one stroke in advance. This allows the drummer to perform within an extreme dynamic range while remaining free of tension.

The use of the level system will allow the drummer to execute patterns which were previously out of reach. Most importantly, the level system will aid the drummer's performance in a manner that works with both the body and the rebound of the stick.

The level system was pioneered by George Lawrence Stone, a prominent figure in drum education. Mr. Stone was the principal instructor at the Stone Drum and Xylophone School in Boston, Massachusetts. It was there that Stone taught his prize student, Joe Morello, who refined the system while utilizing the rebounding strokes as taught by his other teacher, Billy Gladstone. Mr. Morello in turn passed the information along to his pupils, who include Danny Gottlieb, Steve Fidyk, and the author of this book.

This book will prove to be a valuable aid to the drummer who has experience on the instrument but wishes to further develop a natural technique. It can also be an important tool for the beginning student learning the techniques and rudiments of drumming. Rudimental and orchestral drummers should both find the applications of this book to be very practical. Drumset players will not only benefit from the hand exercises, but also from the drumset exercises in the last chapter.

As this is a guide book, the examples are short as to draw attention to the task at hand. The review sections are similar to what may be seen in real-life situations or method books. It is advised that the reader apply the natural technique concepts in this book to his or her performance material and method books.

The concepts in this book have been passed down to me by my teachers, Steve Fidyk and Joe Morello. I have used these concepts in teaching and performances throughout the years and have yielded wonderful results. I hope this book will aid in your development of technique and allow for an effortless execution of the concepts discussed.

Dedication

I would like to thank my teacher and friend, Steve Fidyk, for his guidance and encouragement in regard to both my playing and this book. I would like to thank Robert Nowak for guiding me through the early stages of my development. I must also thank Larry Hart, who did an amazing job with the photos and clip art. Special thanks to Vic Firth and Sabian for their great products and neverending commitment to education. Most importantly I thank my parents, Bill and Anna Marie, for supporting me through all my musical endeavors, and my wife, Jennifer, for her love and encouragement. This book is dedicated to my grandmother, Carmella Lamana, who never stopped believing in me, and my teacher, Joe Morello, a musical genius and true inspiration.

Technique

Technique is often labeled in terms of speed, endurance, and power. These are not definitions of technique, only results. The term itself when referenced to drumming is the ability to direct the sticks using the energy provided by the hands along with the facility to control and manipulate the stick after the rebound has occurred. Through the use of this book, the drummer will learn to work with the body, not against it.

Technique is also thought of in terms of grip. There are many drummers, however, who use varying grips while still allowing the stick to work to their advantage. The techniques in this book may be practiced with any number of grip variations. No matter which grip is used, it is essential to have a loose enough hold on the sticks. Too much pressure will hinder the rebound and ultimately produce tension in the body.

It is suggested that the drummer experiment with grip variations, utilizing the techniques which work and disregarding those that hinder the rebound or add unnecessary tension. It is advised that the student seek out a well-informed teacher who has both knowledge of natural technique and experience applying it to performance situations.

The Metronome

The use of a metronome is highly recommended for the study of this book. The drummer must know how to use the metronome effectively to get the most of his or her practice time. A few key points are listed below.

- Start the exercise at a slow tempo so each stroke can be observed for correct technique. After proficiency has been gained, increase the tempo gradually. Stay at each metronome marking until it is appropriate to move up in tempo.

- If tension occurs, slow the tempo down.

- Keep a record of metronome markings. This will help to guage progress and aid in effective practice.

- Spend time with the metronome clicking the subdivisions of the beat such as eighth notes, sixteenth notes, and triplets. This will help to ensure rhythmic accuracy.

Notation Key

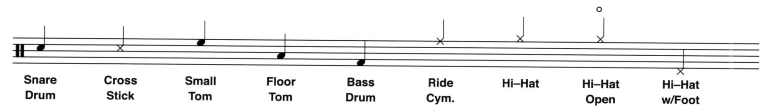

| Snare Drum | Cross Stick | Small Tom | Floor Tom | Bass Drum | Ride Cym. | Hi–Hat | Hi–Hat Open | Hi–Hat w/Foot |

The Rebounding Stroke

Many drummers throw the stick down and stop the rebound. This requires them to pick up the stick before making another hit. Therefore they are using two motions and only getting one sound. The momentum is also broken during the process.

The foundation of the level sysyem is the rebounding stroke, where the stick starts in an upright position. It is thrown down and rebounds back to the starting position. The stick is not brought back by the hand, but by the rebound—similar to bouncing a basketball. Therefore, one motion is used to achieve one sound. To accomplish this, the hand must be loose and free of tension. The full and tap strokes are the main rebounding strokes.

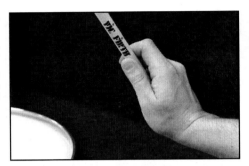
The stick starts in a raised position...

strikes the drum...

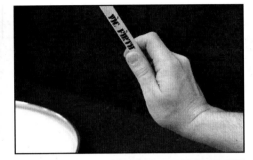
and immediately *rebounds* back to the starting position.

The Rebounding Stroke
Traditional Grip

Most photos and illustrations in this book incorporate matched grip, where both hands grip the stick in the manner shown above. The exercises in this book may also be practiced using traditional grip as well.

Traditional grip is an alteration of the non-dominant hand. Its origin dates back to the early days of marching snare drums. The drum was held close to the body by a sling that spanned over the shoulder, producing a severe angle of the drum. The non-dominant hand was altered to accommodate the angle of the drum. Many drummers continue to use this grip today. It is suggested that you experiment with both traditional and matched grip.

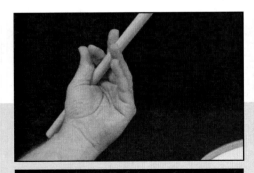
The stick starts in a raised position...

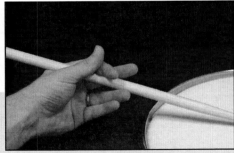
strikes the drum...

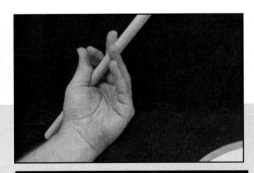
and immediately *rebounds* back to the starting position.

The Level System

If all strokes were played at the same volume, the music would be very uninspiring. Fortunately, drummers have a vast array of dynamics at their disposal. Accents are also helpful in adding to the excitement of the music. The stick height, or level, will be the main factor in achieving the desired volume. This level system will provide a method to easily perform accents and shift from one dynamic to another.

Hand-Level Diagrams
Single-Hand Diagrams

The following diagrams are used to explain the starting and ending positions of the level system.

Tap Position

Full-Stroke Position

Starting-Position Diagrams
Combined-Hand Diagrams

For the level system to work properly, the sticks must start in the correct position.
The book uses diagrams, before dynamic and accented examples, to ensure a correct starting position.

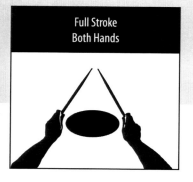

Full Stroke
Both Hands

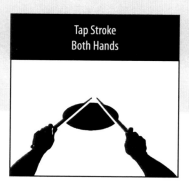

Tap Stroke
Both Hands

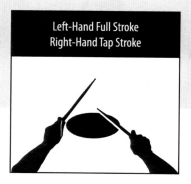

Left-Hand Full Stroke
Right-Hand Tap Stroke

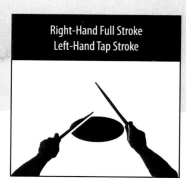

Right-Hand Full Stroke
Left-Hand Tap Stroke

Full Strokes

The full stroke starts with the tip of the stick pointing upward.
It rebounds back to the same position.

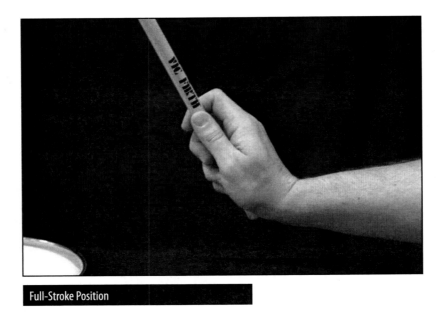

Full-Stroke Position

The full stroke is the power stroke used for loud notes, as well as accents.
It is also a wonderful tool for warming up. It allows the muscles to be stretched
and warmed, and also helps to develop a reflex action in the wrists.

It is used for accents or loud passages.

Throughout the book, the abbreviation "F" is used to signify the use of the full stroke.

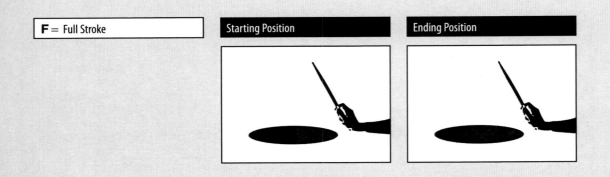

| **F** = Full Stroke | Starting Position | Ending Position |

Practice the following exercise using:

A. Right hand only   **B.** Left hand only   **C.** Unison strokes   **D.** Alternated strokes

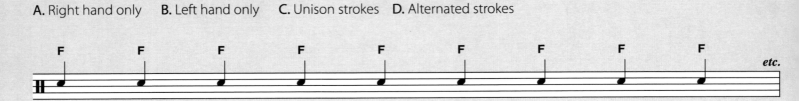

Full Strokes
Dynamics

Dynamics are degrees of volume. While the drum by nature tends to be a loud instrument,
it is necessary to have control at all volume levels. There are two main degrees—loud and soft.
They are designated by abbreviations printed below the staff.

$\boldsymbol{p}$ = *piano* (soft) $\boldsymbol{f}$ = *forte* (loud)

The level system allows the drummer to achieve identical volume from each hit.
Using a natural approach, play the loud dynamic from the full-stroke level
(tips of the stick pointing upward). Remember to allow the stick to rebound back
to the original position. The sticks should have the same beginning and ending height,
regardless of the rhythm being played.

The following exercises should start with both hands in the full-stroke position.

Tap Strokes

The tap stroke is the normal playing position for the drummer.
The stick will start approximately 3 to 6 inches from the drum
(depending upon the desired volume) and rebound back to the same position.

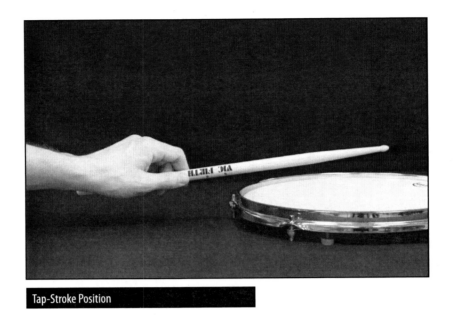

Tap-Stroke Position

The tap stroke is used for unaccented notes and moderate volume passages.

The tap stroke is often referred to as a half stroke.
Throughout the book, the abbreviation "t" is used
to signify the use of the tap stroke.

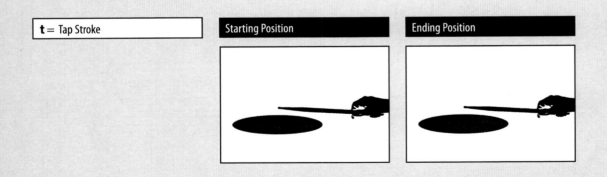

t = Tap Stroke   Starting Position   Ending Position

Practice the following exercise using:

A. Right hand only   **B.** Left hand only   **C.** Unison strokes   **D.** Alternated strokes

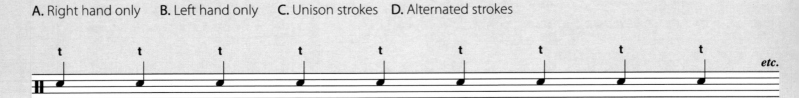

Tap Strokes
Dynamics

To achieve a soft dynamic level, play the strokes from the low end of the tap position (tips of the stick about 3 inches or less from the head). Remember, the sticks will begin and end in the same position.

The following exercises should start with both hands in the tap position.

Upstrokes

The upstroke will allow the drummer to transition from a soft to a loud note. The stroke will start from a tap position and end in the full-stroke position. This requires the hands to be very loose. The wrist may help a little to bring the stick up, but it should be in one motion while the rebound is occurring. The upstroke should be the same volume as the tap strokes.

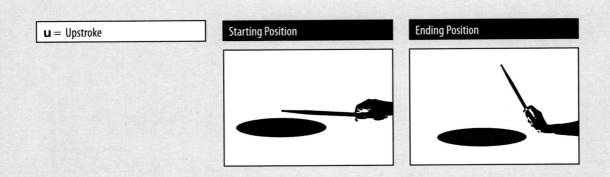

A very effective practice method when learning the level system is to isolate the hands, perfecting one hand at a time.

The following exercises do not repeat.

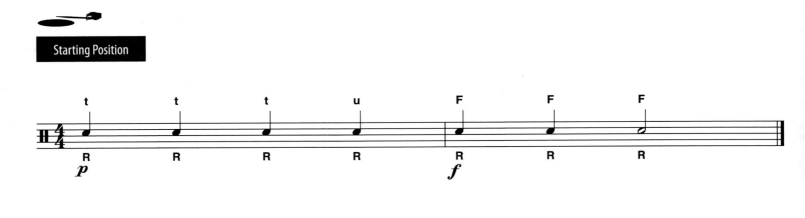

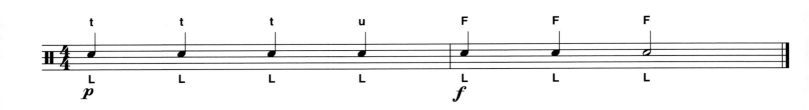

Downstrokes

The upstrokes facilitate the transition from a soft to a loud dynamic. At times, the drummer will need to do the opposite. This requires the use of the downstroke. The downstroke will start from a full-stroke position. Instead of rebounding back to the starting position, the back fingers will come in slightly to absorb the shock of the attack and keep the stick down. It is important not to squeeze or choke up on the stick. A little pressure is all that is required.

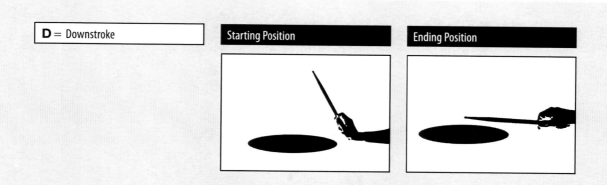

The downstroke is also an important stroke for accents and rudiments. Practice each hand separately before attempting an alternated sticking.

The following exercises do not repeat.

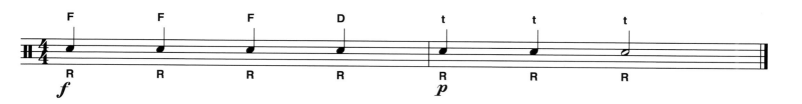

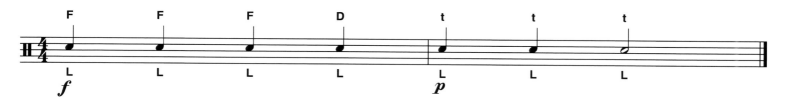

Fine Tuning Dynamics

As previously stated, there are many dynamic expressions.

Below is a comprehensive list:

ppp	=	*pianississimo* (extremely soft)
pp	=	*pianissimo* (very soft)
p	=	*piano* (soft)
mp	=	*mezzo piano* (moderately soft)
mf	=	*mezzo forte* (moderately loud)
f	=	*forte* (loud)
ff	=	*fortissimo* (very loud)
fff	=	*fortississimo* (extremely loud)

The stick height will produce the dynamic that is required.
The velocity in which the stick is thrown will *fine tune* the dynamic.

- *Mezzo forte* will be played with the sticks in the upper end of the tap position.
  It will also be attacked with less velocity than the louder hits.

- *Mezzo piano* will be executed with a slightly lower hand position than ***mezzo forte***.
  The stroke will also have less velocity.

- *Pianissimo* and ***pianississimo*** will be played low to the drum and with less velocity.

- *Fortissimo* and ***fortississimo*** will be played from the full-stroke position and with greater velocity.

Changing Dynamics Quickly
Applying the Tap, Full and Upstroke

The following exercise starts at a mezzo forte dynamic level and immediately switches to fortissimo. The mezzo forte will be played using tap strokes and the fortissimo using full strokes. The upstrokes allow for a smooth transition between dynamics.

The following exercises do not repeat.

Here are some examples applying the technique to changing rhythms.
Begin each exercise with both hands in the tap position.

Make sure to follow the stickings so the motions work correctly.

Changing Dynamics Quickly
Applying the Tap, Full and Downstroke

The downstroke is again utilized. The exercises on this page do not repeat. They should start with both hands in the full-stroke position.

Starting Position

Changing Dynamics Gradually
The Crescendo

The term *crescendo* means to increase in volume. The sticks must gradually elevate toward the full-stroke level. This will result in each hit being higher, and therefore louder, than the preceding stroke.

The *crescendo* can be abbreviated *cresc.* It is also notated by lines increasing in width (◁———◁). Practice the following exercises slowly at first, watching the motion of your hands.

The following exercises do not repeat. They should start with both hands in the tap position.

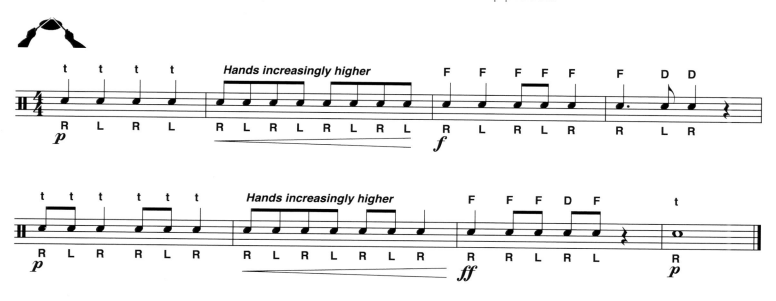

For *piano*, remember to start with the hands down.
Don't start the *crescendo* until the second measure.

In the next example, be careful not to achieve the louder dynamic too soon.
Let each hit come back just slightly further than the previous one.

Changing Dynamics Gradually
The Decrescendo

To *decrescendo* means to decrease in volume.
It is also known by the abbreviation *decresc.* or shown as two lines closing together (⟩).
Diminuendo is a synonymous term and is abbreviated *dim.*

With the *crescendo*, the stick rebounded slightly higher than the starting position.
For the *decrescendo*, the opposite occurs. The wrist and fingers will allow the stick
to rebound to just below the starting position. This is similar to a downstroke,
but the motion is not as severe.

The following exercises do not repeat. They should start with both hands in the full-stroke position.

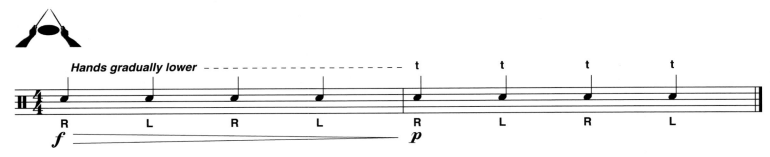

The following example utilizes a long *decrescendo*.

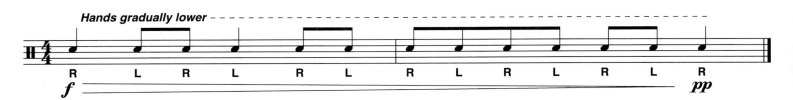

In this example, do not *decrescendo* softer than the *mezzo piano* dynamic.

Changing Dynamics
Hand Motions

The following exercises utilize all the strokes you've learned so far. To review, there are four basic strokes:

- Full Stroke "**F**" — used for loud notes in succession

- Tap "**t**" — used for soft notes in succession

- Upstroke "**u**"— used to transition from soft to loud notes

- Downstroke "**D**" — used to transition from loud to soft notes

Remember that the stick height will produce the dynamic that is required.
The velocity in which the stick is thrown will *fine tune* the dynamic.

The following exercises do not repeat. They should start with both hands in the tap position.

In the following exercise, the last two notes of the second measure should be played as downstrokes to prepare for the dynamic change. Make certain the notes in the last measure are of the same volume and stick height. A common mistake is to **crescendo** through the *f*.

Dynamics
Control and Endurance Exercises

Control is developed through the accuracy of rhythms and motions. Endurance is achieved through repetition. Repeat each measure many times before moving on. If tension occurs, stop and relax. Then, restart the exercise at a slower tempo or with fewer repetitions. Tension will hinder control.

The motions inside the parentheses are to be used only to transition to the next exercise. When repeating, play the motions outside of parentheses.

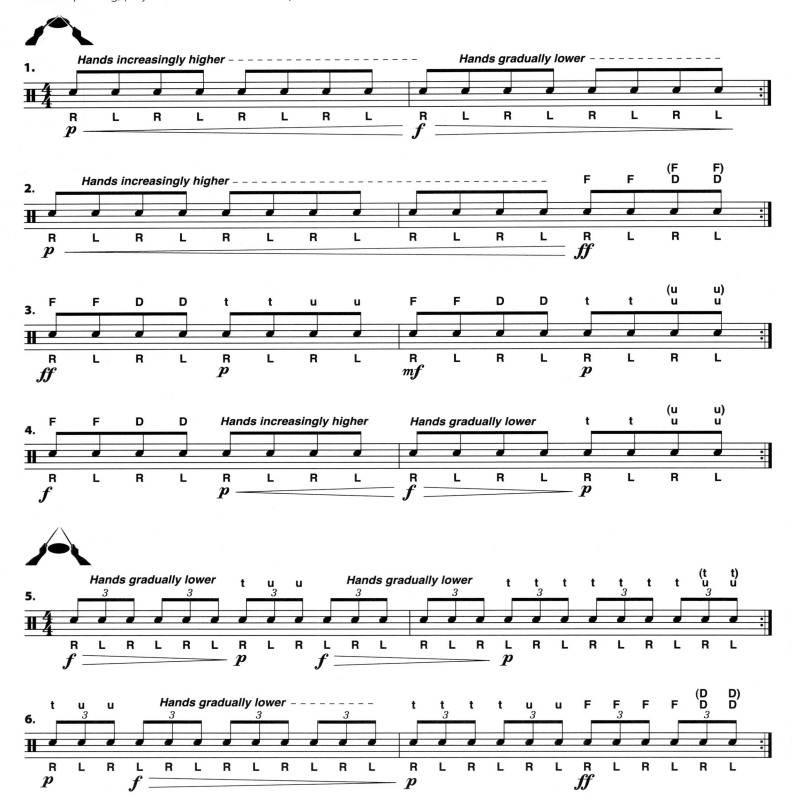

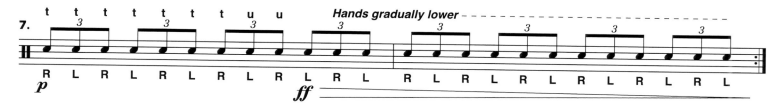

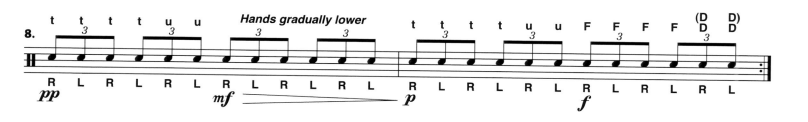

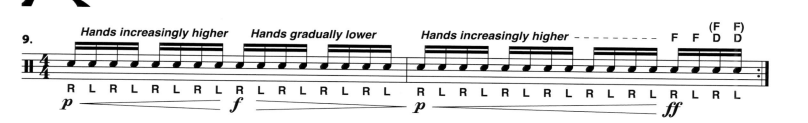

Accents

An accent (>) is an extra emphasis placed on a note. To accomplish this, play the accented note slightly louder than the surrounding notes. The accent should add to the musical phrase. One common mistake is to play the accent too forcefully, therefore breaking the flow of the music.

The same series of techniques used for dynamic changes will be applied to accents. Take a look at the following exercise:

Notice the accent on beat 3. A common error is to press into the drum from the same level as the unaccented notes. This will create an accent, but may also create tension in the hand and a poor sound from the drum. The level system utilizes the following techniques:

- Start in the tap-stroke level.

- Prepare for the accent by playing an upstroke on beat 2.

- Allow the hand to rebound all the way back. It will then be in position for beat 3.

- Beat 3 will be played as a downstroke, since the following right-hand stroke is not accented. Accent heavily in practice, lighter in performance.

 Exercises 1–4 start with both hands in the tap position.

In the following exercise, the left hand utilizes the upstroke and downstroke.

The next example utilizes the full stroke and downstroke in the left hand.

Many times a measure will contain accents in both hands.

In the following exercise, the right hand must start in the full-stroke position while the left hand is in the tap position.

The next exercise begins with the left hand in the full-stroke position and the right hand in the tap position.

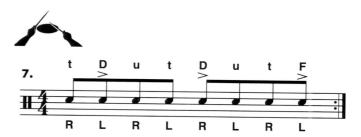

In the following exercise, beat 4 must be a full stroke to prepare for the accent on the repeat.

In the following exercise, both hands start in the full-stroke position.

The next exercise in ⁶⁄₈ time uses an alternating down-up-tap pattern.

The following example shifts the accent from the right hand in the first measure to the left hand in the second measure. Notice how the motions fascilitate the accent shift.

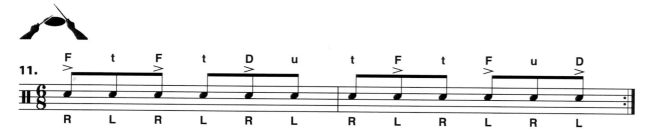

Accents
Control and Endurance Exercises

As stated earlier, motions inside the parentheses are to be used only to transition to the next exercise. When repeating, play the motions outside of the parentheses. Repeat each exercise until comfort and accuracy are achieved.

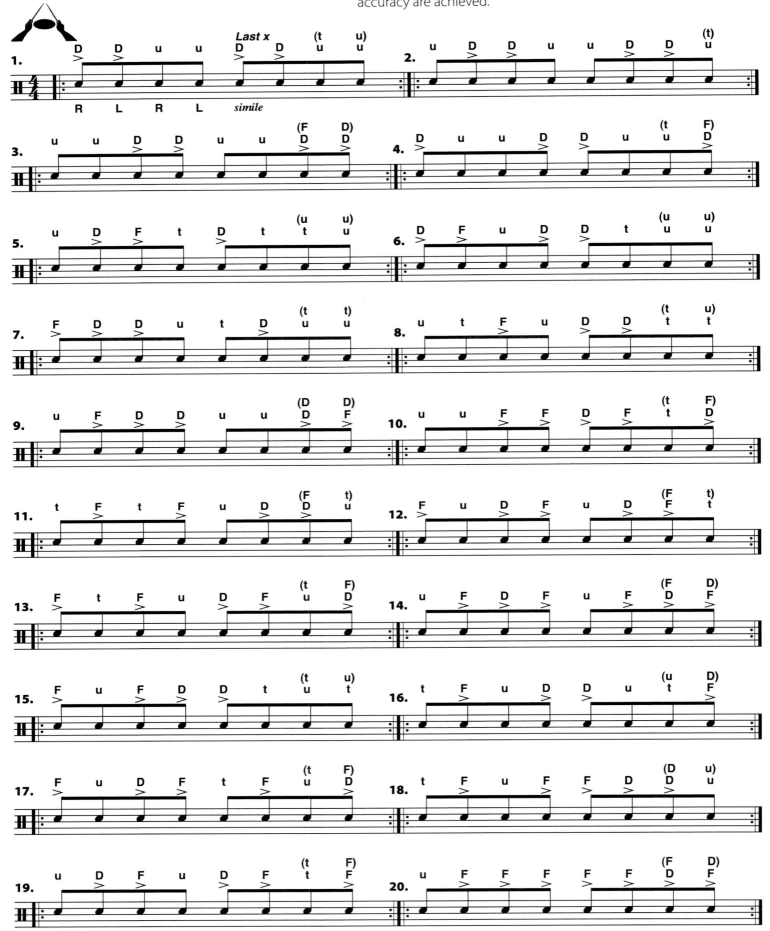

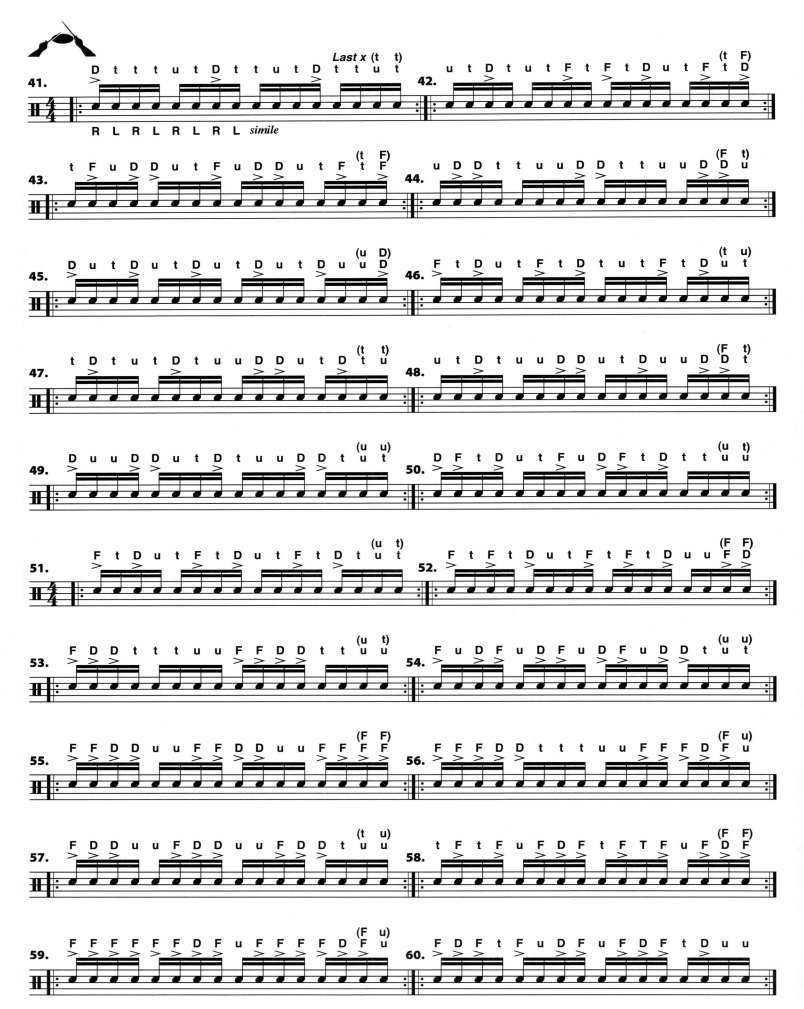

Rudimental Motions
Diddle Rudiments

Rudiments are the basic sticking, accent, and rhythmic patterns of drumming. They are traditionally used in marching band or drum-corps style playing. The standardized stickings make the marching drum line visually cohesive. They also aid in the execution of difficult rhythms. Rudiments have also found their way into drumset patterns and solos.

Rudiments were originally compiled by the National Association of Rudimental Drummers. The Percussive Arts Society later added to the list for a total of 40 rudiments. That is the standard list that most drummers use. There are, however, hybrid or combination rudiments that are being used by many drum corps today.

Paradiddle
The paradiddle is performed using a down, up, tap, tap pattern.

The exercises on pages 27 and 28 start with the right-hand full-stroke position, and the left-hand tap position.

Double Paradiddle
The double paradiddle is a six-note grouping that alternates much like the paradiddle, but with two extra single strokes. Be sure to use the motions.

The double paradiddle can be thought of as 16ths in $\frac{3}{4}$ time.

Or in $\frac{4}{4}$ time.

The double paradiddle is often played with an extra accent on the third stroke.

Triple Paradiddle
The triple paradiddle consists of four single strokes preceding a paradiddle.

Paradiddle-Diddle

The paradiddle-diddle is a six-stroke rudiment. It is similar to the double paradiddle but does not alternate. The accomplished drummer should be able to play the rudiment starting with either hand.

Rudiments are often used in combinations.
Here is a pattern based on two double paradiddles and one single paradiddle.

The following combination uses a paradiddle-diddle followed by a double paradiddle.

The next exercise uses a triple paradiddle, double paradiddle, three paradiddles, and ends with a double paradiddle.

Sometimes the rudiment does not change, but the rate at which it is played changes.
This is the case in the following examples.

Paradiddle-Diddle

In the next example there are four single paradiddles.
Two are played as sixteenth notes, and two are played as sixteenth-note triplets.

Single Paradiddle

Rudimental Motions
Accent Variations

Drummers often alter the accent structure of the rudiments.
It is not uncommon to encounter several rudimental accent variations within a single piece of music.

Accent Variation — Paradiddle
In the following exercise, the accent is shifted by one sixteenth note per measure.
Note that the motions change to accommodate the new accent scheme.
This is especially apparent on beat 4 of every measure.

The following exercises start with the right-hand full-stroke position, and the left-hand tap position.

The accent can shift within a single measure as seen below.

Flams

The flam is a rudiment that is comprised of a main note and a grace note. The grace note precedes the main note and is much softer in volume. To understand how the rudiment should sound, say the word, "flam." The "f" sound is representative of the grace note and the "lam" represents the main note.

Practice the right-hand flam first. Place the right hand in the full-stroke position, with the tip of the stick pointing straight up. The left hand should be an inch or two from the drum.

This is often referred to as a low stroke. It can be thought of as the lower end of the half stroke's range. Release the pressure in the fulcrum of the left hand so the stick drops to the drum. Let it bounce back but do not allow any further rebounds from that hand. The right hand will strike soon after, playing a full stroke. Remember, the full stroke will return to its starting position. Avoid the "pop" sound that results from both hands hitting simultaneously.

Right-Flam Position

Left-Flam Position

Below is the right-hand flam. The left hand plays the grace note. The right-hand motion plays a full stroke.

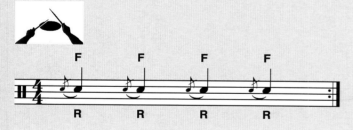

The left-hand flam has the left playing full strokes on the beat. The right hand plays the grace note slightly before the beat. Remember to keep the grace notes close to the drum.

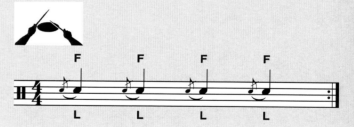

For consecutive right or left flams, use full strokes as the main note. If a flam is followed by a non-flammed note, use a downstroke for the main note. In the following exercise, the downstroke prepares the hand for the non-flammed notes while the upstroke anticipates the flam on the repeat.

The next exercise starts with the left hand in the full-stroke position to prepare for the flam on the "and" of beat 1.

Alternating Flams
Flam Rudiments

The flam, as a rudiment, traditionally alternates. In other words, if the first flam is a right flam, the next will be a left. To execute the alternating flam, the grace note of the flam is played as an upstroke. The main note is played as a downstroke. Make sure there are two distinct stick heights—low and high. A common mistake after playing a few alternated flams is to keep both sticks in the "grey area" somewhere in the middle.

Rudiment – Flam

Rudiment – Flam Tap
The Flam Tap is an alternated flam followed by an extra tap. The tap is played with the hand that is already close to the drum.

Rudiment – Flam Accent
The Flam Accent is a three-note grouping which alternates. The motion is a down flam followed by an upstroke and a tap.

Flam rudiments can be used in combination with each other. This example uses four flam accents followed by flam taps.

Rudiment – Flam Paradiddle
The flam paradiddle is a paradiddle with a flam at the beginning of each phrase.

Rudiment – Flamacue
The flamacue uses the alternating flam to prepare for an accent on the second beat. That accent is played as a downstroke and followed by an upstroke to prepare for the next flam. Even though the flams are not accented, they should still be played in the full-stroke position but with a bit less velocity.

Rudiment – Flam Drag
The flam drag is similar to the flam accent. The exception is the middle beat, as it is a double. The second stroke of the double is an upstroke. This may seem awkward at first, but it is an important technique in rudimental performance.

This exercise is notated using triplets. It shifts between flam accents and flam drags.

After the flam rudiments have been mastered with a high flam stroke, the height of the flam may be brought closer to the tap position. The grace note will still be much closer to the drum. This will aid in the execution of the rudiment at faster tempos, as well as facilitate softer dynamics.

Flam Rudiments
Control and Endurance Exercises

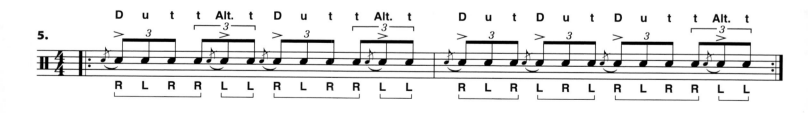

7.
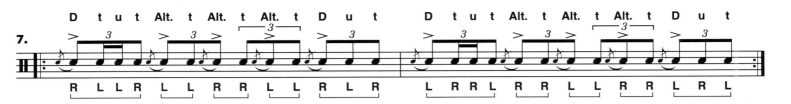

8.

9.

10.

11.

12.

13.

Drum Rolls
Open-Roll Applications

The open roll consists of exactly two hits per hand. The desired sound can be likened to that of a machine gun. Open rolls are numbered according to the total number of hits, including the ending tap. Practice the following exercises slowly at first, concentrating on the motions and sound.

Rudiment – Five-Stroke Roll – Alternates

The five-stroke roll as a rudiment alternates. It often starts on the downbeat. The first double for each five-stroke roll consists of a tap and an upstroke. This prepares the hand for the upcoming accent.

The five-stoke roll can also start on the "and."

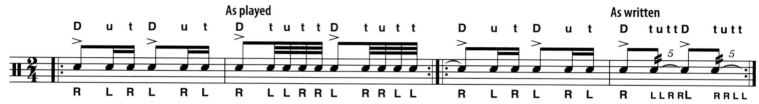

Rudiment – Seven-Stroke Roll – Does Not Alternate

The seven-stroke roll as a rudiment does not alternate. Practice the roll with both a right- and left-hand lead.

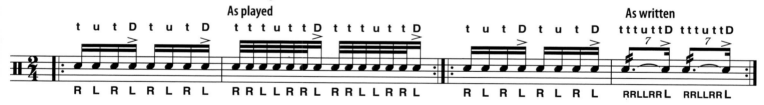

The seven-stroke roll may also start on the second sixteenth note and end on the following downbeat.

Rudimental pieces sometimes ask for a seven-stroke roll to span over the length of an eighth note. In this case, the roll must be pulsed as a doubled sixteenth-note triplet.

In the following example, the seven-stroke roll starts on the downbeat.

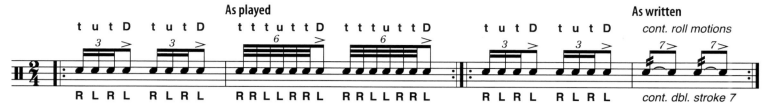

Rudiment – Nine-Stroke Roll – Alternates

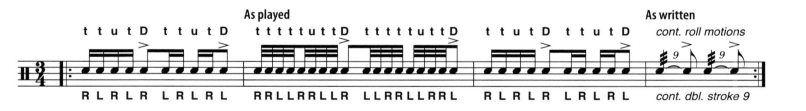

Rudiment – Thirteen-Stroke Roll – Alternates

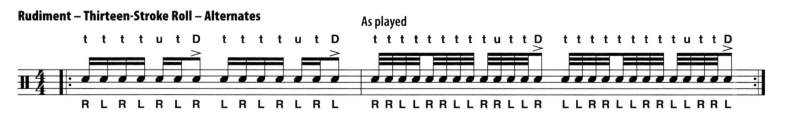

The thirteen-stroke roll can start on the beat as previously shown.
It can also start on the "and" as in the following example.

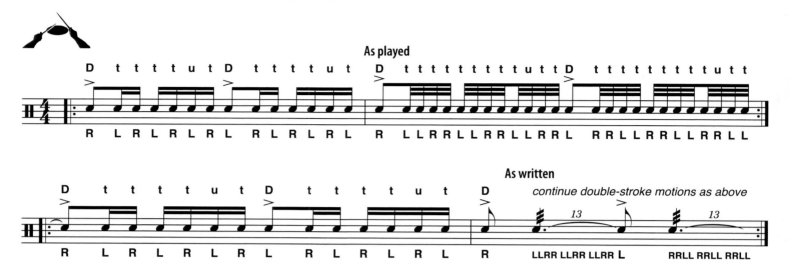

Rudiment – Seventeen-Stroke Roll – Alternates

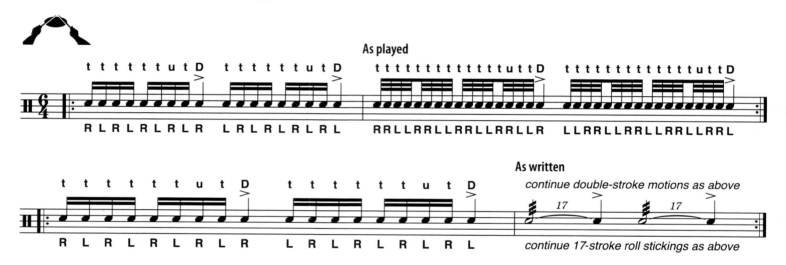

The following exercise utilizes all the rolls discussed in this section. Measure one contains a thirteen-stroke roll. Measure two uses both five- and seven-stroke rolls. Measure three has a nine-stroke roll. Measure four completes the exercise with a seventeen-stroke roll.

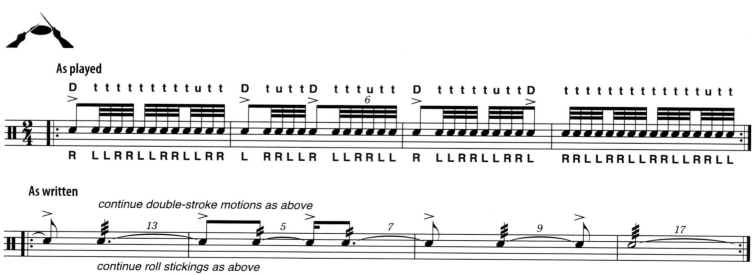

The basic rolls have been covered. There are still others to be addressed at a later time.

The Drag

As previously discussed, the flam has one grace note. The drag is similar to the flam, but incorporates two grace notes. The grace notes will be performed as controlled double strokes (as in the open roll). It should be noted that the drag may also be played closed, or as buzzes. However, for the purpose of learning the level system, all drags in this book will be played open.

In the first example, the grace notes are played with the left hand and the main notes with the right. In a practice situation, experiment with the right hand starting as far back as possible and the left hand close to the drum. In a performance situation, the hands may start lower depending upon the dynamic needed.

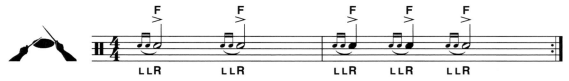

Practice the above exercise again.
This time, reverse the sticking to obtain a left-hand lead.

Alternated Drags (Level-System Notation)
The grace notes of an alternated drag consist of a tap and an upstroke. The main note of the drag is a downstroke. It is abbreviated as "Alt."

Drag Rudiments

Rudiment – Drag – Alternates

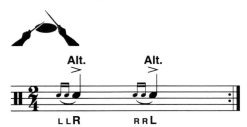

Rudiment – Lesson 25 – Does Not Alternate
Start with the right hand in the full-stroke position and the left hand low to the drum. Since the main note of the drag is an unaccented note, the grace notes must be considerably lower in height. Also practice with a left-hand lead, reversing the sticking.

Lesson 25 can also start with the drag. In this example, start with the right hand in the tap position and the left hand noticeably lower.

Rudiment – Drag Paradiddle #1 – Alternates
Start the drag paradiddle #1 with the right hand in the full-stroke position, and left hand close to the drum head.

Rudiment – Drag Paradiddle #2 – Alternates

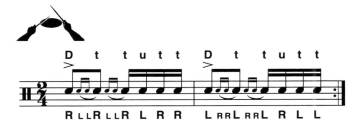

Rudiment – Single Ratamacue – Alternates

The single ratamacue may also begin on the eighth note.

Rudiment – Double Ratamacue – Alternates

Rudiment – Triple Ratamacue – Alternates

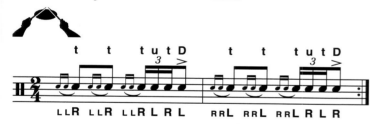

Rudiment – Single-Drag Tap – Alternates

In the single-drag tap, the alternated motion prepares for the upcoming accent. Start with the right hand in the tap position and the left hand noticeably lower. Again, the double on the left will consist of a tap and an upstroke. Allow the upstroke to come back to the full-stroke position. This will enable a strong accent on the "and."

Rudiment – Double-Drag Tap – Alternates

In the double-drag tap, the right hand will start from the tap position and the left hand will be noticeably closer to the drumhead. The grace note immediately preceding beat 2 will have to rebound back to the full-stroke position, similar to the single-drag tap.

Flam Rudiments Revisited

The most common flam rudiments were studied in an earlier chapter. It is now time to introduce the remainder of the flam rudiments.

Single-Flammed Mill – Alternates

The single-flammed mill is similar to a flam paradiddle, except the double is now at the beginning of the rudiment.

Flam Paradiddle-Diddle – Alternates

The flam paradiddle-diddle is similar to the paradiddle-diddle. The flam version, however, does alternate.

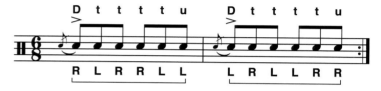

Rudiment – Swiss Army Triplet – Does Not Alternate

The Swiss army triplet is very useful for tempos that are too fast for execution of the flam accent. This is because the swiss army triplet contains only two hand hits in succession (including the grace note), as opposed to the flam accent which contains three.

Practice the Swiss army triplet with both a right- and left-hand lead.

Rudiment – Pataflafla – Does Not Alternate

The pataflafla is comprised of four notes with a flam placed on the first and last note. Practice also with a left-hand lead.

Rudiment – Inverted Flam Tap – Alternates

The inverted flam tap uses a continuous down-up motion that will take some time to perfect. Practice slowly at first. Increase the speed only after a comfort level is achieved.

Rolls Revisited

The basic roll values were discussed in a previous chapter.
This section will address the six-, ten-, eleven-, and fifteen-stroke rolls.

Odd number rolls such as the five-, seven-, and nine-stroke roll consist of a series of double stokes followed by a tap.
The six- and ten-stroke rolls contain two taps. Since these rolls do not alternate, practice them with both a right-
and left-hand lead.

Rudiment – Six-Stroke Roll – Does Not Alternate

Start with the right hand in the full-stroke position and the left hand in the half-stoke position (or lower).
Every double will consist of a tap and an upstroke.

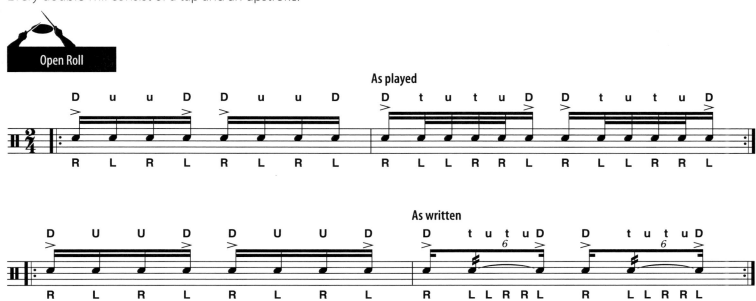

Rudiment – Ten-Stroke Roll – Does Not Alternate

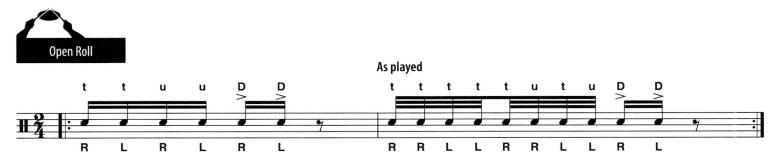

Rudiment – Eleven-Stroke Roll – Does Not Alternate

The eleven-stroke roll is the same duration as the ten-stroke roll but only has one accent.

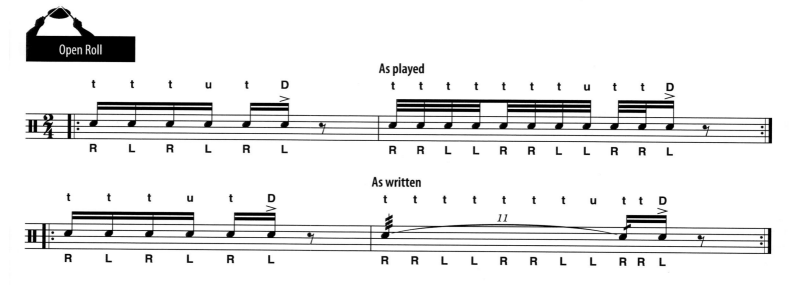

Rudiment – Fifteen-Stroke Roll – Does Not Alternate

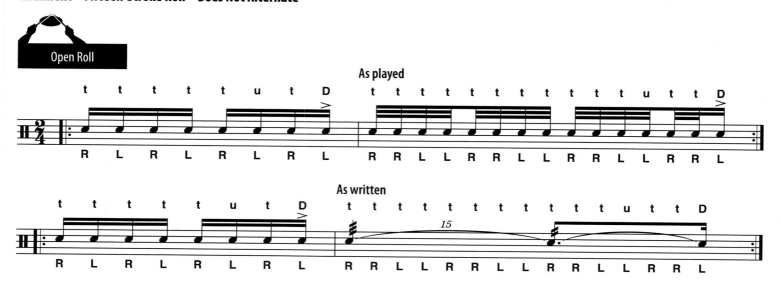

The fifteen-stroke roll often starts on the "e" of the beat.

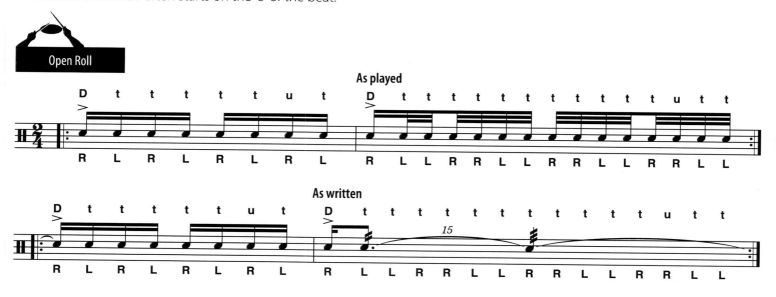

Drumset Applications
Right-Hand Accents

The level ststem may be easily adapted for performance on the drumset. The first area to be examined will be the hi-hat. In contemporary rock drumming, the hi-hat is often accented to solidify the time feel.

Right-Hand Part – Eighth Note Hi-Hat Rhythms

In the following exercises, the hi-hat is played using eighth notes. The downbeats are accented. The first measure isolates the hi-hat part utilizing the motions of the level system.

In the second measure, the hi-hat part is used in context with a common bass and snare drum pattern. *The motions in this section refer to the right hand only.*

RH Starting Position

Eighth-Note Rock – Right-Hand Part

Eighth-Note Rock – Complete Pattern

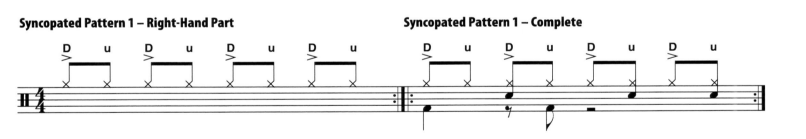

Syncopated Patterns – Eighth Note Hi-Hat Rhythms
Don't allow the right-hand motions to change if the bass or snare patterns are altered.

Syncopated Pattern 1 – Right-Hand Part

Syncopated Pattern 1 – Complete

Syncopated Pattern 2 – Right-Hand Part

Syncopated Pattern 2 – Complete

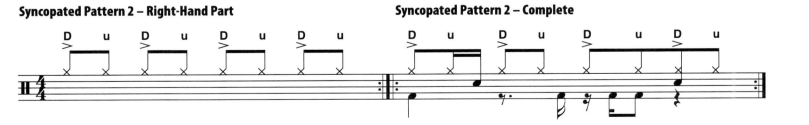

RH Starting Position

Hi-Hat Accent Variations
The following exercise is based on the disco rhythm. The accents will occur on the "ands."

Disco – Right-Hand Part   **Disco – Complete Pattern**

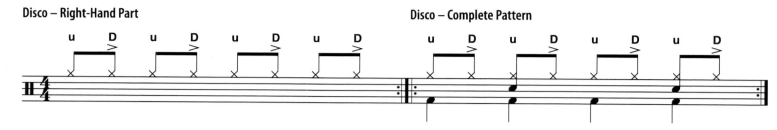

The following pattern substitutes a hi-hat accent in place of a snare drum backbeat.
This is often seen in eighth-note ballads, although it can also be used at faster tempos.

Eighth-Note Ballad – Right-Hand Part   **Eighth-Note Ballad – Complete Pattern**

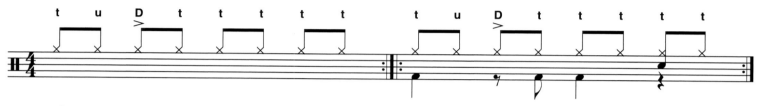

RH Starting Position

Shuffle Pattern
Similar to the eighth-note rock patterns, the shuffle may also have accents on the downbeats.

Shuffle Pattern – RH Part   **Shuffle Pattern – Complete**

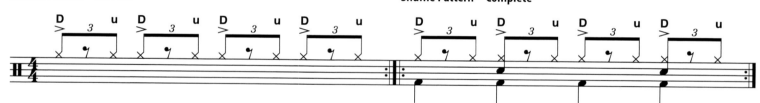

Triplets
Below is a common accent pattern for triplets.

Triplet Pattern – RH Part   **Triplet Pattern – Complete**

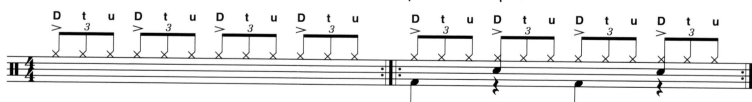

In the following exercise, the accent pattern outlines, or implies, quarter-note triplets.

Triplet Variation – RH Part   **Triplet Variation – Complete**

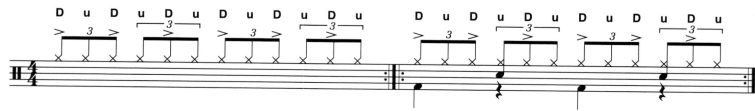

RH Starting Position

Right-Hand Part – Sixteenth-Note Hi-Hat Rhythms

Below is a sixteenth-note based hi-hat pattern.
Accents are often used to outline the underlying eighth-note pulse.

Sixteenth-Note Pattern 1 – RH Part   **Sixteenth-Note Pattern – Complete**

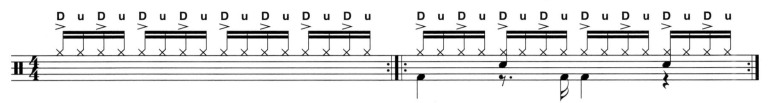

As stated earlier, the right-hand accents should not
change regardless of the snare or bass drum rhythms.

Sixteenth-Note Pattern 2 – RH Part   **Sixteenth-Note Pattern 2 – Complete**

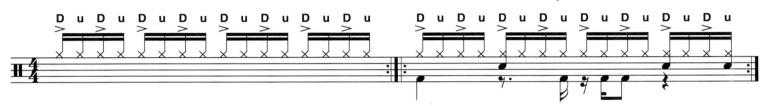

Eighth- and Sixteeth-Note Combinations

The following exercises contain common hi-hat variations.

Eighth and Sixteenth Combination 1 – RH Part   **Eighth and Sixteenth Combination 1 – Complete**

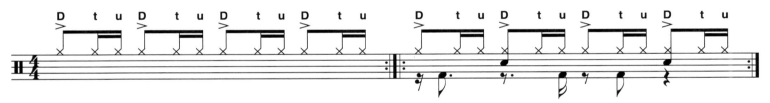

Eighth and Sixteenth Combination 2 – RH Part   **Eighth and Sixteenth Combination 2 – Complete**

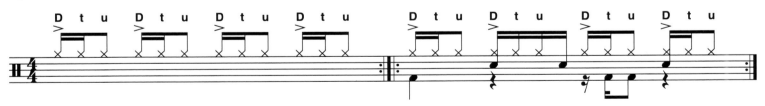

RH Starting Position

Hip-Hop

Hip-hop patterns can be thought of as swung sixteenth and eighth-note combinations.

Hip-Hop – RH Part   **Hip-Hop – Complete**

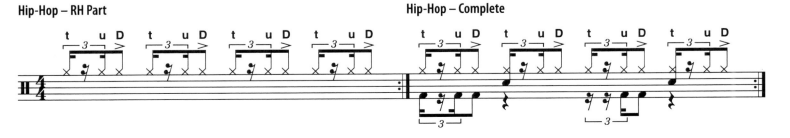

Drumset Applications
Left-Hand Accents

The accent pattern may also appear in the left-hand part. This is the case in many rock rhythms. To create a groove that is true to the style, play the unaccented notes at a pianissimo to piano dynamic. The accented notes should be performed at a forte or fortissimo dynamic. *The motions in this section refer to the left hand only.*

LH Starting Position

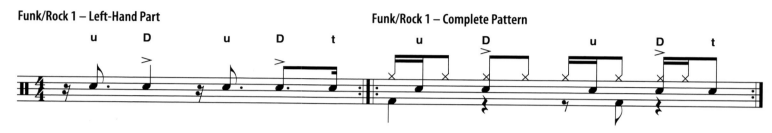

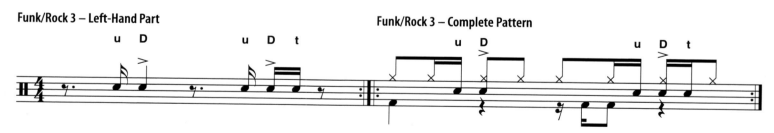

Practice the above patterns as written, with unaccented eighth notes in the right hand. Also experiment with hi-hat accents as seen on pages 41–42.

The Shuffle
The shuffle pattern (as previously seen on page 42) may also be played with the left hand. In the following pattern, the right hand plays the downbeats while the left hand performs the shuffle pattern.

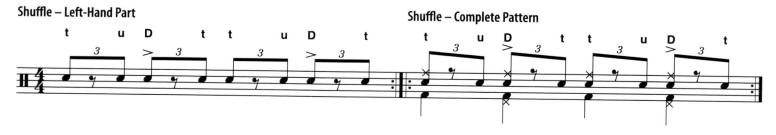

Half-Time Shuffle
The half-time shuffle has been credited to Bernhard Purdie.
It has also been popularized by John Bonham and Jeff Porcaro.

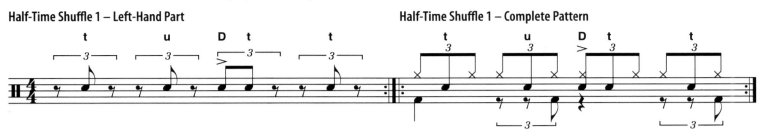

Below is another left-hand variation for the half-time shuffle.

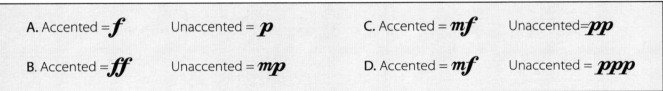
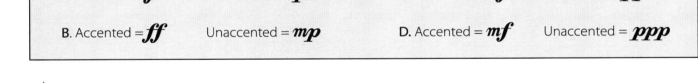

Jazz

The ability to switch between soft notes and accents is a necessary requirement for the jazz drummer. In the following exercises, experiment with the degrees of volume for the accented and unaccented notes. A few examples are listed below.

A. Accented = *f* Unaccented = *p* **C.** Accented = *mf* Unaccented = *pp*

B. Accented = *ff* Unaccented = *mp* **D.** Accented = *mf* Unaccented = *ppp*

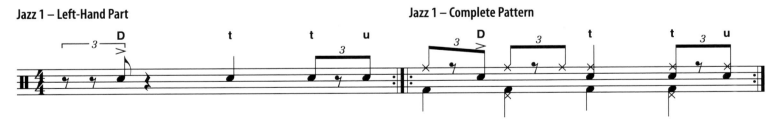

Jazz 3 – Left-Hand Part

Jazz 3 – Complete Pattern

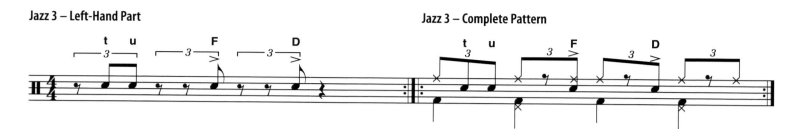

Jazz Samba

The left-hand part of the jazz samba utilizes all of the motions (taps, downstrokes, upstrokes, and full strokes).

Jazz Samba – Left-Hand Part

Jazz Samba – Complete Pattern

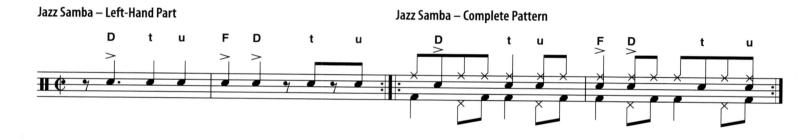

Songo

The songo, an Afro-Caribbean rhythm, has a very interesting left-hand accent pattern.

Songo – Left-Hand Part

Songo – Complete Pattern

Drumset Applications
Right- and Left-Hand Accents

Country Train Beat
The country train beat is to be played with an alternated sticking, starting with the right hand.

Second Line – New Orleans
This second-line example also utilizes an alternated sticking. For a variation, the sixteenth notes on beat 4 can be played as an open five-stoke roll. The eighth notes should be slightly swung.

Krupa Style Tom Beat
This accent pattern is reminiscent of Gene Krupa's style. It should be played using swung eighth notes. The sticking should be alternated as in the last two examples.

Batucada – Hand Part
The batucada is a popular Brazilian pattern.

Batucada – Complete Pattern

The next pattern is an interesting variation on a calypso beat.

Calypso – Hand Pattern

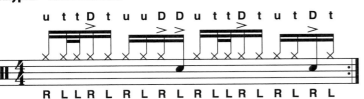

Calypso – Complete Pattern

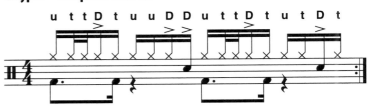

Drumset Applications
Transcriptions

This section includes a number of transcriptions. While the original artists may have used any number of techniques in their performances, this book will apply the level system to attain the balance between accented and unaccented notes.

Oops	Drummer: Peter Erskine	Artist: Steps Ahead	Album: *Modern Times*

This pattern is a repetitive five-note grouping with an accent on the last note. Below is the hand pattern followed by the transcription. The right hand plays the bell of the ride cymbal.

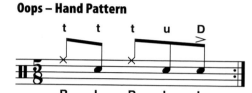

Oops – Hand Pattern

Soul Vaccination	Drummer: David Garibaldi	Artist: Tower of Power	Album: *Tower of Power*

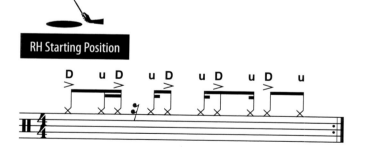

Complete Pattern
Hands—Top Staff
Feet—Bottom Staff

| **Hot Fun** | Drummer: Steve Gadd | Artist: Stanley Clarke | Album: *School Days* |

This is the groove that Steve Gadd played toward the end of the piece (approx. 2:07).
The right hand plays the hi-hat while the left hand plays the snare drum. It may also be played open-handed, without crossing hands. This is a method that Steve Gadd often employs.

| **Fire on the Bayou** | Drummer: Zigaboo Modeliste | Artist: The Meters | Album: *Fire on the Bayou* |

Hand Pattern

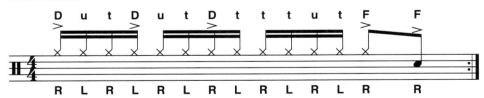

Complete Pattern

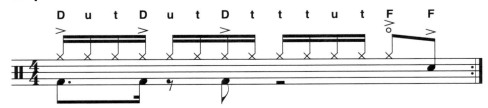

Drumset Applications
Fill and Solo Concepts

Six-Stroke Roll

The six-stroke roll is a popular rudiment to apply to the drumset.

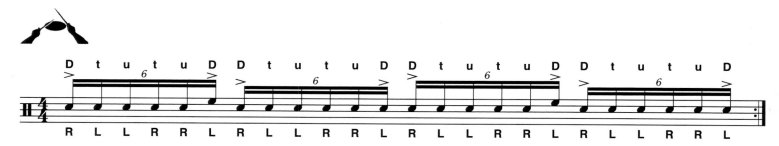

RLL RLL RL

The following accent pattern outlines a common rhythm that may be used for fills or solos.

Blushda

The blushda is a popular solo phrase that utilizes flams and drags.

Here are more solo patterns that incorporate the level system.

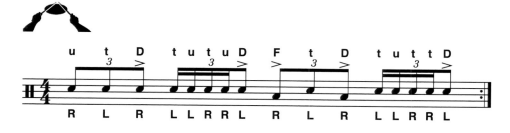

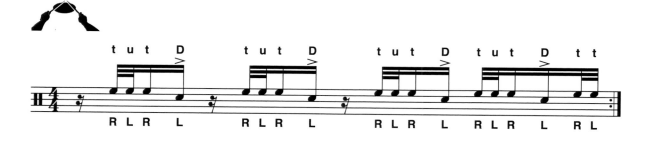

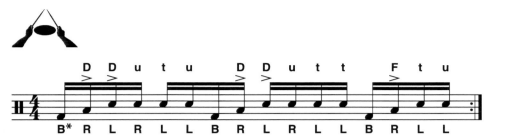

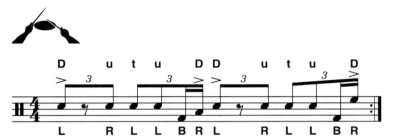

The next set of exercises incorporate accents phrased in one grouping with the left hand, and another with the right hand. This style of soloing is credited to Joe Morello.

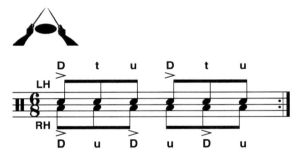

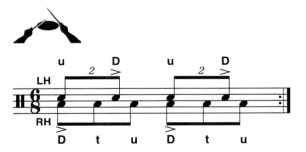

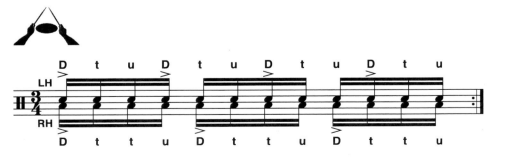

*B = Bass Drum

Recommended Study

This book is meant to be a foundation for the development of natural technique. The next step is application. The drummer is encouraged to apply the principles in this book to his or her practice routines and performance situations. Below is a list of books which may be used in the application of the techniques.

Technique

Stick Control – George Lawrence Stone
Master Studies – Joe Morello
Master Studies II – Joe Morello
Accents and Rebounds – George Lawrence Stone
Roll Control – Joel Rothman
Odd Meter Calisthenics – Mitchell Peters
Accent on Accents – Elliot Fine and Marvin Dahlgren
Artificial Techinque – Joel Rothman

Technique Videos and DVDs

Joe Morello: Drum Method 1 – The Natural Approach to Technique – Joe Morello
Joe Morello: Drum Method 2 – Around the Kit – Joe Morello
Natural Drumming: Lessons 1 & 2 – Joe Morello and Danny Gottlieb
Natural Drumming: Lessons 3 & 4 – Joe Morello and Danny Gottlieb
Natural Drumming: Lessons 5 & 6 – Joe Morello and Danny Gottlieb

Reading Studies and Etudes – Basic

Syncopation – Ted Reed
Vic Firth Snare Drum Method, Book 1: Elementary – Vic Firth
Vic Firth Snare Drum Method, Book 2: Intermediate – Vic Firth
Primary Handbook for Snare Drum – Garwood Whaley
Musical Studies for the Intermediate Snare Drummer – Garwood Whaley
Rolls, Rolls, Rolls – Joel Rothman
Snare Drum Duets – Thomas A. Brown
Concert Solos for the Intermediate Snare Drummer – Garwood Whaley
Solos and Duets for Snare Drum – Garwood Whaley
Podemski's Standard Snare Drum Method – Benjamin Podemski

Reading Studies and Etudes – Rudimental

N.A.R.D. Drum Solos – Compilation
The All-American Drummer – Charley Wilcoxon
Modern Rudimental Swing Solos for the Advanced Drummer – Charley Wilcoxon
William F. Ludwig Collection Drum Solos - Compilation
The Rudimental Cookbook – Edward Freytag
Rudimental Primer for the Snare Drummer – Mitchell Peters
14 Modern Contest Solos for Snare Drum – John S. Pratt

Reading Studies and Etudes – Orchestral

Modern School for Snare Drum – Morris Goldenberg
Rhythmic Patterns of Contemporary Music – Garwood Whaley and Joseph M. Mooney
Advanced Snare Drum Studies – Mitchell Peters
Contemporary Studies for the Snare Drum – Fred Albright
The Solo Snare Drummer – Vic Firth
Recital Solos for Snare Drum – Garwood Whaley
Classical Percussion – Arthur Press
Portraits in Rhythm Complete Study Guide – Anthony J. Cirone
The Snare Drum in the Concert Hall – Al Payson

Drumset – General Drumset Methods

Drumset S.M.A.R.T. Book – Steve Fidyk
Advanced Concepts – Kim Plainfield
The Drummer's Complete Vocabulary as taught by Alan Dawson – John Ramsay
Creative Coordination for the Performing Drummer – Keith Copeland
Drumset Warm-Ups – Rod Morgenstein
The Drum Perspective – Peter Erskine

Drumset – DVDs

Set-Up and Play – Steve Fidyk
Shed Some Light – Steve Holmes

Reference Material

The Complete Percussionist – Robert B. Breithaupt
Snare Drum Roll and Rudiment Interpretation – Gary J. Olmstead
Teaching Percussion – Gary D. Cook